The Castle to My Heart

Mary Hale

www.WeAreAPS.com

Copyright © 2018 by Mary Hale

All rights reserved. No part of this publication may be reproduced, stored in a retrieval system, or transmitted, in any form or by any means, electronic, mechanical, photocopying, recording or otherwise, without the prior permission of the publishers.

ISBN: 978-1-945145-41-4

APS Publishing
2653 S. Lawndale
Chicago, IL 60623
847-942-6135
www.WeAreAPS.com

Table of Contents

Part 1......................................5
The Walls of Deception

Part 2......................................17
The Vision Revisited

Part 3......................................27
The Vision Explained

Part 1

The Walls of Deception

There is an old saying, "Into each life some rain must fall." I am a true believer of this because I have found some days are wonderful and some days are not so wonderful, but we all must live and go through life one day at a time. Deception is a stronghold that we all deal with every day, whether in our home, at work, school, etc. Some of us can deal with it wholeheartedly, and some of us can't or don't.

So, the question is, do we live life, or do we survive through deception? Not wanting to deal with what life dishes out to us. Thinking that it will work out all by itself.

We are deceived first naturally, then spiritually.

In the natural, the word deception means, fraud, cheat, trickery, chicanery, deviousness, slyness, wiliness, guile, bluff, lying, pretense, treachery. Spiritually, deception causes us to have irrational thoughts because it affects the heart.

When we become involved with people and everyday life, we are forced to deal with other people's wants and needs as opposed to our own wants and needs. Do we get involved with other people's problems, or do we just deal with our own? If that person can't see things our way, do we walk away? Do we assume they must do as we say do – handle things the way we have from our own experiences? This is when our control issues start.

I say this because we must look at our own heart and reasoning before we can even touch on the deception of others. Do we control our feelings, or do we try to control the other person's feelings? Whether we yield to that other person or deceive ourselves, we do it so that we can have things our way.

Deception holds us captive because it is a spiritual wound in our life. The fruit of deception is isolation, excluding ourselves from others, being overly dominating, controlling and spreading false accusations. There is also the feeling of abandonment and loneliness, not feeling wanted or needed, being unable to fit in, being a victim, and having the fear of rejection.

What happens with deception is we begin to blame others because we feel it is never our fault; deception does not allow us to see our own faults. We begin to complain about unnecessary things and become judgmental.

We start to spread gossip and hold unforgiveness in our heart, which causes a lot of illnesses because unforgiveness means we are unable to let go of what is ailing us. We hold unforgiveness and it eats at our heart and soul.

There is heaviness and restlessness and we become angry, frustrated and full of resentment toward ourselves and others, which brings about bitterness and more frustration to ourselves. This is a cause and effect because it is spiritual, and believe it or not, these actions bring on sickness such as high blood pressure because of the hidden anger that some of us are unable to release.

Some of us hide our feelings in alcohol and drugs to try to cope with the deception we feel within. It affects all of us in way whether it be attention seeking, through exercise, video games or pornography. These are walls of deception. With these walls come depression and anxiety.

In the world we live today, anything goes, and our children suffer. The internet is the biggest deception because children can go on the internet and see everything, we as parents try to keep from them. The relationship between parent and child is the most important one because children learn from their parents.

Today, children learn from their parents and other influences that are sometimes not acceptable in our homes. So, with that comes a lot of experimenting and some of us never make it back to the reality that our minds were not readily developed from what we were exposed to or what we have learned.

In a lot of relationships people are secretive. Sometimes, it is because we are ashamed of our past and present mistakes, or embarrassed because we deal with fear of what others such as our mates, family and friends may so or do.

Self-deception allows us to believe lies that we tell ourselves through false thoughts and we get into our feelings and have our own ideas about different ways of life. We feel that in our mind what we believe is true.

This can be very dangerous in any relationship because we are deceived by our own thoughts that make us uneasy as we try to protect our own self image at the expense of others. We can't be honest in any relationship for fear of being laughed at or judged, and no longer desire to have that relationship.

I believe that deception leads to a form of rejection. I think when people feel rejected, it is the number one cause and effect of deception. I am not trying to justify deception, but rejection comes with deception.

Our thoughts have a way of overtaking reality, so we hide from ourselves and others through deception. Deception brings fear and false accusation. We began to doubt things that concern our lives because we are misinformed by our own perception of life.

Then we become angry and hostile toward others. With that deception comes worry and anxiety and we start to feel guilty from the doubt and hostility. We go through life with regret from believing the lies that have been in minds. Then we are discouraged, disappointed and full of regret from the time that was lost and some of us sink into depression. We separate ourselves from family and friends for fear of rejection because of our ignorance of being self-absorbed and self-deceptive.

So, what happens with those thoughts of deception is that we stray away from anyone that tries to get close to us and those that really care enough to be honest. We become hostile and reject anything and everything that the other person tries to offer for fear of being embarrassed. Then, we become more absorbed in our public image rather than our relationships with no regard for the other person's feelings.

This leaves the other person unfulfilled, unloved, and pushed to the side. There is no trust, there is no love and the relationship has ended. Some of us stay in these relationships and try to pretend that everything is okay. This is another form of self-deception.

Through life, we miss out on our opportunity to grow in these relationships whether it is with a mate, family member, or friend because we are afraid to share ourselves in a meaningful connection with others because of low self-esteem. Low self-esteem makes us afraid to commit to anyone. Some of us are not even aware that we have low self-esteem and that is another form of where the deception is located.

Low self-esteem is when we are in fear of failure and are over zealous about being negative of other people's accomplishments. Why? Because of our own fears regarding ourselves. We feel unworthy and unable to achieve like others. This is possibly because we have been told this from others sometime in our lives.

The fruit that flows from our heart will show the deception on the inside because bitterness, a hot temper, and the need to control will come from the issues of life.

Self-love cannot be experienced when we have a broken heart that has not been healed. The broken heart is like a disease or condition that appears when those who were supposed to love us did not. This happened as a result of harmful actions that were done mentally or physically; they neglected to act in loving ways you needed.

But today is a new day, a new beginning, a new mercy. God has the final say, and if he can create a way of escape for me, I know that He will do the same for you!

Part 2

The Vision Revisited

In a vision, I saw myself walking through a garden. The garden was dark and gloomy as if it had no life and was deserted. There was a pedway that took me through the garden of wilted flowers. As I looked from a distance, I saw a castle that looked like it had been abandoned. As I got closer, there were tall trees covering something. I could see that it was dark and gloomy; there was no light. It was as if no one lived in the castle.

As I began to approach the castle behind the trees, I saw a large red heart standing in front of the castle. It was almost as tall as the castle, but it had been hidden by the trees. The heart had a crack in the middle. It had a flow of blood running out of it slowly, and it was swollen. I had a lot of questions running through my head. I thought to myself, "Why is a broken heart in front of a castle? Why was it red, yet the castle had no color"? I never gave a thought that this might not be a place to enter because I felt so comfortable being in this place.

I walked past the heart toward the castle. The castle was about a block away. I avoided getting blood on my shoes because I somehow went around the heart. As I was walking, I could not get over the fact that the heart was that big. But, why was the heart cracked and bleeding? Who would put a heart in front of a castle? What did the heart represent? There were a series of questions I had going on in my head, but all I could do was look at the heart from a distance as I was walking.

Once I turned, I saw that the castle was now about a half block away from the heart. When I arrived, I entered the castle. It had no doors inside, just tall ceilings and walls, and it was made of bricks. There were no furnishings or pictures; it looked dusty and empty with cobwebs. It was so cold and dark. It looked as if it had been empty for a long time. There was a balcony leading upstairs. There were stairs on both sides of the entry with no windows.

There were about 15 stairs on each side of the balcony. As I went up the stairs, I entered the second floor of the castle. There were about five or six empty rooms, but no doors or windows. This castle was empty. It looked as if no one ever lived in it. Straight ahead was another set of stairs that led to a large room with no windows – just a brick wall. I thought to myself, "This must have been a hiding place". I went back downstairs and noticed that there was no other entrance or exit aside from where the red heart was located. So, I went outside the castle and looked around.

There was no way around the castle.

The bricks would not allow me to pass, so I went back into the castle. As I entered, I noticed an open room under the stairs. This opening led to another large room, which had a window, however, I was unable to open it. It was a large glass sealed by the bricks.

I looked out the window and saw a beautiful garden with a lot of colorful flowers. There was another heart in the garden that was gold. It was not as large as the red heart, and it was glowing and beautiful. I stood amazed at the heart and tried to understand why the red heart was blocking castle, yet the gold heart was in the back of the castle. I really didn't understand what was going on, so I went back upstairs.

In my vision, I gave no thought to what was happening. Instead, I began to label and assign each room, which seemed to represent my life and feelings about the incidents that occurred as far as relationships with family, friends, co-workers, and others who affected my life. I even categorized each room for every person that was part of my life in the past as well as the present. I assigned each person to a room by labeling their name to the walls of the corresponding rooms.

They were assigned to a room according to where I allowed them to enter. I did not assign them to the room where I thought they would be comfortable because it was my room and my castle. I placed them in the rooms in which I wanted them. These rooms were labeled Hate, Heartache, Disappointment, Pain, and Rejection. The only good room in the castle was underneath the stairs with the window by the gold heart, which was the one place I was unable to enter.

I was on my way downstairs and

heard laughter, but I knew there was no one in the castle but me. I went to the room under the stairs and looked out of the window into the courtyard. There was the gold heart shining and sparkling with my children and grandchildren standing right next to it. They were talking, laughing, and enjoying life. I could tell they loved being close to that heart.

I sat in the room under the stairs looking out at the window of opportunity, but not able to open it. I wondered why they were in the yard, yet I couldn't get to them? I could not find an entry into the garden. There was no door, and I couldn't open the window because it was sealed with bricks. I could not enter the courtyard. I could only see them being happy and enjoying the heart.

Suddenly, it was quiet. I could see them but could no longer hear the laughter. The heart was pumping quite fast; it was happy and excited.

No one else including me could enter the courtyard – only the ones that I saw through the window. It was then that I realized that the red and gold hearts were mine, and the castle I was in was the walls of the foundation that I had built. These were the bricks that I'd laid for many years, which explained why there were spider webs and darkness. These were the bricks that had held me captive for so long regarding my life and the people therein.

Part 3

The Vision Explained

I have gotten past the broken red heart that sat in front of the castle. The healing and restoration have begun. The castle walls are no longer gray. The room under the stairs is a place of new beginnings. I am in my castle that I built from the past of my everyday life. I no longer have rooms without windows, and some of the rooms now have doors. The only way to deal with these walls is to reconstruct them one day at a time. I must tear down, root up, rebuild and release whatever is holding me back.

The wall I was writing about is self-deception. I had to go through the door and open the window to release the past and move on to the future so that the healing could begin.

> When there are no windows of opportunity to the heart and the doors are closed, and there is no circulation, destiny will never breathe...it will die.

The heart refers to the soul of a human being that controls the will and emotions. The heart is the "inner man" (2 Corinthians 4:16).

The heart is the seat of life. It represents love and security. It is the symbol for affection, desire, love and hatred. It is the ability to care for others. The word heart refers to our feelings, will, and intellect. This was why the heart was in the center of the castle.

In the dream, I did not stop at the red broken heart. I bypassed all my feelings, my desires, even the hatred. I went past disappointment, rejection, loss, unpleasant situations and embarrassment – I went past it all.

The broken heart that I first encountered represented brokenness, which I had allowed to dictate my future. Why? Because I never dealt with the issues of life at the present time, so the heart became heavy and it cracked.

The castle represented control, strength and confidence. It represented the situations where I was aware of myself being the powerful influence.

The rooms represented boundaries, or my personal space. These were empty rooms lacking furniture and pictures; they had no paint or color. They represented the need to avoid others, or situations with minimal or no social contact.

This is how I was able to go up the stairs and label the rooms. On each side of the castle were 15 stairs. In the Bible, the number 15 represents Nisan (the first day of the feast of unleavened bread; a day of rest for the children of Israel, which comes after deliverance).

The steps represented problems or situations that required me to take one step at a time. The steps were going up, which represented an achievement, awareness, or understanding. It also represented a struggle or challenge in my emotional state. The courtyard represented experiences, relationships, emotional refuge and comfort.

The gold heart represented something of value – security, freedom, reward, wealth, happiness – something precious. Therefore, I was able to hear laughter, because this was my destiny that God had prepared for my future.

> "Keep thy heart with all
> diligence; for out of it
> are the issues of life.
> Put away from thee a forward
> mouth, and perverse lips
> put far from thee.
> Let thine eyes look right on,
> and let thine eyelids look
> straight before thee.
> Ponder the path of thy feet, and
> let all thy ways be established."
> **Proverbs 4:23-26**

www.ingramcontent.com/pod-product-compliance
Lightning Source LLC
Chambersburg PA
CBHW031944070426
42450CB00006BA/874